# Inflectional Endings

## by Claire Daniel

SCHOLASTIC
PROFESSIONAL BOOKS

NEW YORK • TORONTO • LONDON • AUCKLAND • SYDNEY

Dear Teacher,

Nothing can be more important in the primary grades than instilling in children the joy of reading and teaching them the skills to become successful, lifelong readers. To do this, we must teach children how to unlock the mysteries of print. Reading instruction that includes systematic and explicit phonics instruction is essential to achieve this goal.

Phonics instruction unlocks the door to understanding sounds and the letters or spelling patterns that represent them. Quality phonics instruction engages children, provides opportunities for them to think about how words work, and offers reading and writing experiences for children to apply their developing skills. The playful, purposeful activities in the *Fun With Phonics!* series offer practice, reinforcement, and assessment of phonics skills. In combination with your daily reading instruction, these activities will help to capture the fun and excitement associated with learning to read.

Enjoy!

*Wiley B.*

Wiley Blevins, Reading Specialist

Cover Design: Vincent Ceci, Liza Charlesworth, and Jaime Lucero
Cover Illustration: Abby Carter
Interior Illustrations: Rick Brown

Series Development by Brown Publishing Network, Inc.
Editorial: Elinor Chamas
Interior Design and Production: Diana Maloney and Kathy Meisl

# Contents

# Using "Fun With Phonics"

*Fun With Phonics!* is a set of hands-on activity resource books that make phonics instruction easy and fun for you and the children in your classroom. Following are some ideas to help you get the most out of *Fun With Phonics!*

## Classroom Management

**Reproducibles** Reproducible pages 7–19 offer a variety of individual and partner activities. Simple directions to the children are augmented when necessary by *Answers* or *Game Directions* in the Teacher Notes section on page 29.

**Directions** You may wish to go over the directions with children and verify that they can identify all picture cues before they begin independent work.

**Games** When children play partner games, you may want to circulate to make sure children understand procedures.

## Working with the Poem

A poem on page 6 introduces the phonics elements in this book, inflectional endings. Start by reading this page aloud to children. Duplicate the poem so that children can work with it in a variety of ways:

**Personal Response** Read the poem aloud and have children talk about it. Ask children if they ever lose things that are "right in front of them."

**Phonemic Awareness** Read the poem aloud each day. Ask children to listen for inflectional endings, such as *ing, s,* or *es,* and to raise their hands when they hear such endings.

**Sound to Letter** Write the poem on a chart, and ask children to point to or circle words with inflectional endings.

**Innovation** Ask children to brainstorm ideas for something else that might be missing. Encourage children to retell the poem with the new item.

## Connecting School and Home

The Family Letter on page 5 can be sent home to encourage families to reinforce what children are learning. Children will also enjoy sharing the Take-Home Book on pages 21–22. You can cut and fold these booklets ahead of time, or invite children to participate in the process. You might also mount the pages on heavier stock so that you can place the Take-Home Book in your classroom library.

## Word/Picture Card Sets

Pages 30–31 of this book contain matching sets of Word/Picture Cards drawn from the vocabulary presented in this book. You may wish to mount these on heavier stock as a classroom resource. You may also wish to duplicate and distribute them to children for use in matching and sorting activities. Each child can use a large envelope to store the cards. Each title in the *Fun with Phonics!* series contains a new set of thirty-two Word/Picture Cards.

## Assessment

Page 20, Show What You Know, provides children with targeted practice in standardized test-taking skills, using the content presented in this book in the assessment items. The Observation Checklist on page 32 gives you an informal assessment tool.

Dear Family,

Your child is learning in school about words with inflectional endings.

When an inflectional ending is added to a base word, it changes the meaning of the word. An inflectional ending can make nouns plural, can make adjectives comparative, or can change the tense of a verb. Some inflectional endings are *s, es, ies, er, est, ed,* and *ing.*

You may enjoy sharing some or all of the following activities with your child:

book     books

### Keep a Diary

Encourage your child to keep a diary for a week. At the end of the week, ask him or her to circle any words that have an *s, es, ing,* or *ed* added. Ask if there are any sentences your child would like to share, but keep in mind that the diary is his or her private writing.

### Action Riddles

Children can create riddles for words with inflectional endings about something they are doing now at home or school or something they have done in the past. For example: *This is something I am doing after school. I do it in the water.* (swimming) Write *swimming* and have your child point out the inflectional ending *ing.*

### Reading Together

To practice reading words with inflectional endings, look over your child's Take-Home Book, "Postcards from Camp." Ask your child to point out all the inflectional endings. You may also wish to look for these books in your local library:

Sincerely,

It Takes a Village
by Jane Cowen-Fletcher

The Napping House
by Audrey Wood

# Dad's Glasses

Dad is looking
For his glasses up and down.
"I have looked all over!"
He sighs with a frown.
He looks in the mirror,
His face turns red:
"There they are—sitting
On top of my head!"

Name _____

# The Roads to Camp

Help the bus take the boys and girls to camp.
Say all the words out loud. Circle the words
that mean more than one. Then let the bus follow
these words to get to camp!

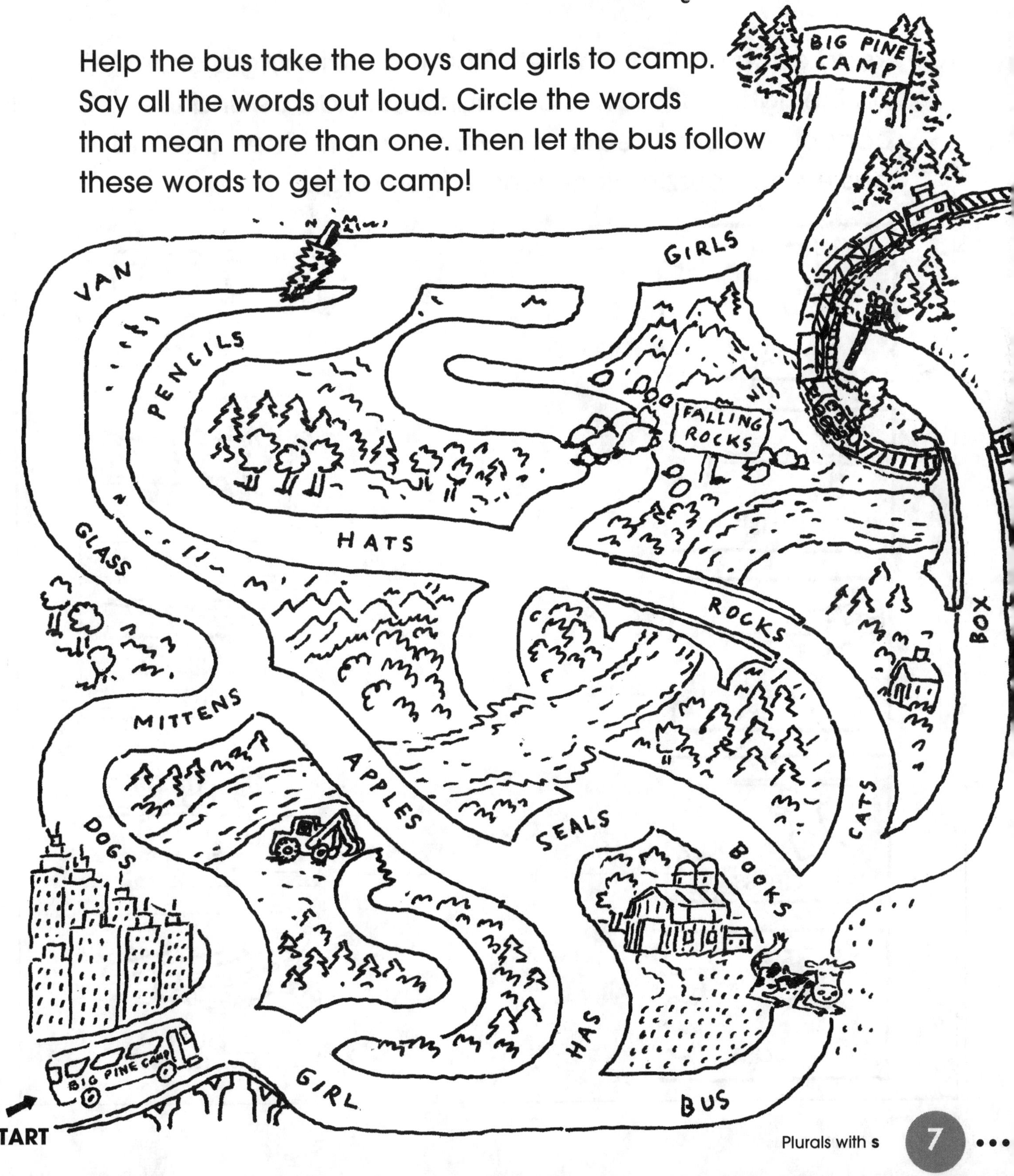

BIG PINE CAMP

VAN

GIRLS

PENCILS

FALLING ROCKS

HATS

GLASS

ROCKS

BOX

MITTENS

APPLES

CATS

DOGS

SEALS

BOOKS

BIG PINE CAMP

GIRL

HAS

BUS

**START**

Name _____

# Puzzle Time

Read each word on the left. Find the matching pictures on the right that show more than one. Add **es** and the correct number to each word on the right. Then cut and paste each puzzle piece where it belongs.

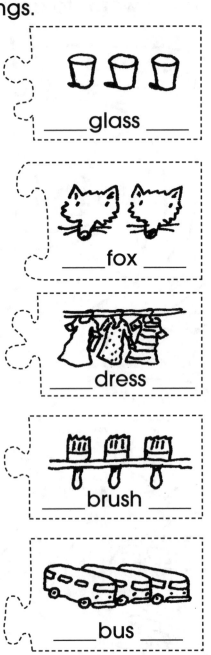

Plurals with **es**

Name _____

# Find the Words

Find the words in the puzzle that name the pictures below. Read across or top to bottom. Circle the words. Then write each word under its picture.

1.  _____

3.  _____

5.  _____

2.  _____

4.  _____

6.  _____

| p | u | p | p | i | e | s | c | i |
|---|---|---|---|---|---|---|---|---|
| e | i | e | b | s | i | e | h | e |
| n | i | d | a | i | s | i | e | s |
| n | e | s | b | b | m | e | r | t |
| i | i | c | i | l | e | s | r | e |
| e | s | l | e | c | s | s | i | e |
| s | s | i | s | w | e | i | e | s |
| e | b | u | n | n | i | e | s | s |

Name _____

# Plural Concentration

Cut out the words. Then play
Concentration with a partner.
Your teacher will tell you how
to play this game.

| | | | |
|---|---|---|---|
| **buddy** | **buddies** | **rock** | **rocks** |
| **candy** | **candies** | **party** | **parties** |
| **box** | **boxes** | **peach** | **peaches** |
| **lunch** | **lunches** | **goat** | **goats** |
| **apple** | **apples** | **pony** | **ponies** |

Plurals with **s, es, ies**

Name _____

# Match Them Up

Look at the pictures. Read the sentences. Draw
a line to connect each picture with its matching
sentence. Then add **s** or **es** to complete each
sentence. HINT: If a word ends in **s, sh, ch, or x,**
you need to add **es**.

1.       Mr. Miller teach _____.

2.       Mom call _____ us for lunch.

3. Jean hit _____ the ball.

4. Ms. Miller fish _____ .

5. The baby sleep _____ .

6. His dog catch _____ .

7. Dad mix _____ the salad.

8. Randy brush _____ his dog.

Name _____

# What Happened Yesterday?

Write **ed** after each word in the box. Then read the clues below and do the puzzle. Use the words you made.

| | | |
|---|---|---|
| help_____ | fish_____ | jump_____ |
| dress_____ | plant_____ | |

## Across

1. Maria ____ all day.

3. The frog ____.

5. Carl ____ a flower.

## Down

2. Tim ____ for school.

4. Karim ____ his mom.

Inflectional Endings © Scholastic Inc.

Name _____

# Ask the Robot

Help Robot speak. Cut out the word strip and place it through the slits. Work with a partner. Take turns asking Robot, "What are you doing?" and moving the strip to get new answers. Write your favorite answer below.

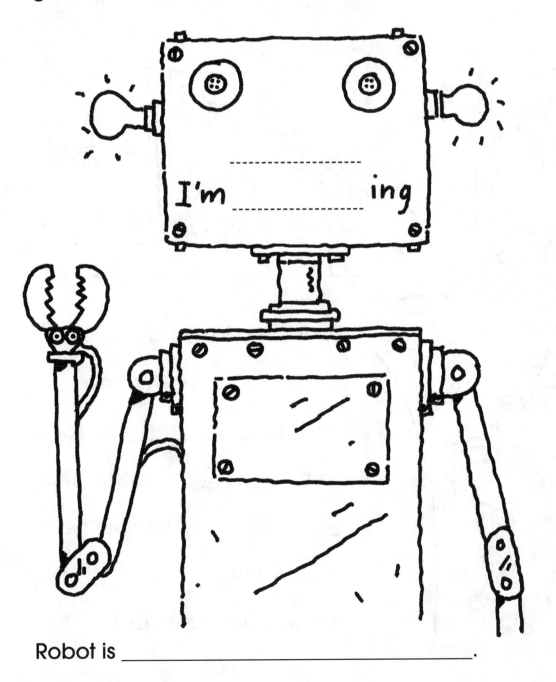

I'm _____ ing

think

look

read

play

sleep

walk

shout

work

speak

Robot is _____.

Name _____

# Ronny's Journal

Look at the scene. Then help Ronny finish her journal entry. Use words from the box.

| tries | flies | studies | carries | dries |

Today is a busy day. Chen

_____ on the steps.

Mrs. Lu _____ the socks.

Tom _____ a kite. Jan

_____ to ride her new

bike. Abby _____ books

home. I like busy days.

Name _____

# Our Day in the Park

Look at the pictures. Then read the sentences that tell about the pictures. Cut them out and paste them where they belong. Circle the endings **ed** or **ing**. Tell the story.

1. Here's what happened on Saturday.

2.

3.

4.

5.

6.

We planned a picnic.    A frog hopped by!    A girl petted a dog.

A man was jogging.    A boy was swimming.

Name _____

# Now and Then Riddles

Read each riddle. Draw a line to the matching picture.
Then write the answer. Use a word from the box.

| waving  skated  raking  danced  baking  riding |
|---|

1. This is what I did on a lake.
   It was a cold day!

   I _____.

2. I do this in the fall.
   It is hard work!

   I am _____.

3. I did this on a stage.
   I did it on my toes.

   I _____.

4. I do this when I go.
   I am saying good-bye.

   I am _____.

5. I went fast when I did this.
   I was on a bike.

   I was _____.

6. It smells good when I do this!
   Yum! It is time to eat!

   I have been _____.

Verbs with **ed, ing**

Name _____

# Tallest and Fastest

Look at the pictures. Read the words. Draw a line to the picture that tells about each word.

1. small
   smaller
   smallest

2. cold
   colder
   coldest

3. fast
   faster
   fastest

4. tall
   taller
   tallest

5. long
   longer
   longest

Name _____

# Mystery Words

**What is missing on the rainiest day of the year?**

Read the clues. For each clue, find one word from the box that means the same. Write the word on the lines. Put one letter on each line. Now read the letters in the tall box from top to bottom. Write the mystery words.

| happier | luckiest | sunniest | thinnest | wetter | windier |
|---------|----------|----------|----------|--------|---------|

1. more **wet**          1. __ __ __ __ __ __

2. most **thin**          2. __ __ __ __ __ __ __ __

3. more **happy**       3. __ __ __ __ __ __ __

4. most **sunny**        4. __ __ __ __ __ __ __ __

5. most **lucky**         5. __ __ __ __ __ __ __ __

6. more **windy**        6. __ __ __ __ __ __ __

Mystery words: _____ _____

Name _____

# Find the Beach Ball

Look at the picture. Find and circle the things named in the box. Then complete the sentence below.

| | | |
|---|---|---|
| the happiest | the smallest | |
| the tallest | the longer | |
| the bigger | the sandiest | |

The ⊛ is under the big _____ hat.

Name _____

# Show What You Know

Look at the picture next to each number. Fill in the circle next to the word that matches the picture.

1.  ○ book
○ books
○ took

6.  ○ biking
○ braked
○ baked

2. ○ dish
○ distance
○ dishes

7.  ○ glass
○ glassed
○ glasses

3. ○ bushes
○ bus
○ buses

8  ○ tall
○ taller
○ tallest

4. ○ pennies
○ pencils
○ penny

9.  ○ fast
○ faster
○ fastest

5.  ○ wishing
○ washing
○ washed

10.  ○ big
○ bigger
○ biggest

Inflectional Endings © Scholastic Inc.

# Postcards from Camp

Dear Mom and Dad,
Day 1
I was on the slowest bus. The tents are hot. Camp is boring. I'm planning to come home.
Ben

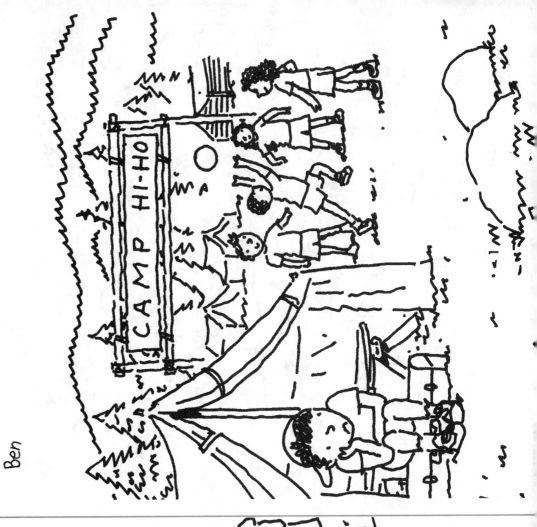

Day 7
Dear Mom and Dad,
The buses are waiting. This has been the fastest week of my life. Next year I want to stay for two weeks. Camp Hi-Ho is the greatest!
Ben

Day 2
Dear Mom and Dad,
Today is even hotter. I guess I will try fishing. I might go hiking later. I'm still planning to come home.
Ben

Day 3
Dear Mom and Dad,
I have two new friends, Sal and Mika. We go swimming every day. We play games. I'm not coming home yet.
Ben

2

3

# Classroom Fun ....••

## Inflectional Endings

### Go Fishing

Write words with *ed* and *ing* endings on fish patterns, and attach a paper clip to each fish. Put the fish in a container, and invite children to go fishing for words with inflectional endings, using a string that has a magnet attached to the end. As a word is pulled out, have the child read it and use it in a sentence. You may also ask him or her to identify the base word for each word pulled out.

This activity can be repeated with base words. Have children fish for a base word such as *stop* or *skate*. Ask them to add *ed* and *ing* to the base word and use each inflected verb in a sentence. See how many fish each child can catch!

### Human Words

Give each child a letter of the alphabet written on large cards or sheets of paper, repeating some letters such as *p*, *b*, *s*, *n*, and *g* as necessary. Call out a base word such as *dish*, *penny*, *book*, or *bus*. Then have children come forward and stand in front of the class with their cards to spell out the word. Say the same words in inflected form (*dishes*, *pennies*, *books*, *buses*) and have children add the inflectional ending, making any necessary spelling changes.

You can also use this activity with verbs. Call out base words such as *drive*, *sleep*, *mix*, and *park*. Then call out the same words with *ed* and *ing* endings, having children make changes as necessary to form the new words.

# Classroom Fun

## Scavenger Hunt

Divide the class up into teams. Then, give children a list like the one below and have them find objects in the classroom that fit each category. They may either collect the items or write the name of a person who has or represents the item.

- ❑ the thinnest pencil
- ❑ the smallest lunch box
- ❑ the biggest notebook
- ❑ the softest sweater
- ❑ the tallest child
- ❑ the thickest book
- ❑ the messiest desk
- ❑ the happiest smile
- ❑ the longest shoe
- ❑ the heaviest coat
- ❑ the cleanest shoelace
- ❑ the muddiest shoe

After fifteen minutes, call the groups together and ask them to show each item they found. For each category, decide which group's item wins, and award a point for each. The group with the most items wins the game.

## The Best Day of My Life

Invite children to write or dictate a story called "The Best Day of My Life." Encourage them to illustrate the story with a drawing. Tell them that because this day has already happened, their action words should be past time words. After children finish writing, have them circle words that end in *ed* and *ing*. Then have children read their stories aloud.

## Make a Counting Book

Read counting books with the class, such as *Ten Black Dots* by Donald Crews or *Ten, Nine, Eight* by Molly Bang. Then invite children to create their own class counting book. Before they begin, have them agree on how high they want to count and what items they want to count. Then let individual children or pairs of children each write and illustrate one page. Have them caption each item as shown.

3 sandwiches

## Bean Bag Game

On a piece of butcher paper, draw circles. Inside each circle, write a different verb, such as *bake, race, jump, stop, wag, climb, cry*. Have children form teams. Have teams take turns having a member toss the beanbag onto a circle. Ask the team to add *ed* and *ing* to the word and write the resulting words on chart paper. Each word the team spells correctly earns the team a point. The team with the most points at the end of the game wins.

# Wordmaker Cards

Divide the class into groups and duplicate the Wordmaker Cards on page 28 for each group. Have children cut out the cards and use them to make as many words as they can by adding *s, es, ed, ing, er,* and *est.* Show them how to double the final consonant when necessary, to cover final *y* with *i* before adding an ending, and to cover final *e* with the ending when adding an ending to words ending with *e.* As children form each word, have them spell it aloud. Have one child (or an aide) record the word for the group. See how many words each group can come up with in a ten-minute period.

# Mural: Things We Like to Do

Invite children to create a mural of things they like to do on weekends. Depending on the season, children will suggest many ideas. List the ideas on the chalkboard. Then, divide children into groups and supply them with markers and large sheets of butcher paper. Have them plan how they will show themselves doing what they like to do. After the murals are complete, supply stick-on labels and have children label each action they illustrated. Check that they have spelled words with inflectional endings correctly. Have each group share its mural with the class.

# Word Shapes

Draw six empty word shapes on the chalkboard for words like these: *dancing, jogging, jumped, wishing, looked,* and *fishes.* Use words that have different shapes. Then write the matching words on the chalkboard in random order. Ask six volunteers to each fill a shape with the letters that spell one of the words.

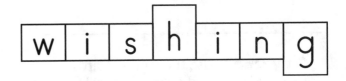

# Word Builder Chart

On the chalkboard create a three-column chart with the following column headings: *Base Word, ed, ing.* Write the following words in the first column: *look, brush, wish, help, dress.* Have children write each word with ed in the second column and with *ing* in the third column. A similar chart can be used to practice words that compare.

# Instant Activities

**What Am I Doing?** Write words like these on index cards. Have partners choose one apiece and keep it a secret: *baking, skating, raking, biking, racing, dancing, smiling, sneezing, skipping, jogging, fishing, brushing, parking, helping, working.* Each child can act out his or her secret word as the partner guesses the action.

**Only One?** Use the Picture Cards for *books, boxes,* and *babies.* For each card, have a volunteer identify the picture and tell whether the word means *one* or *more than one.* Then have another child write the word that names only one. Have him or her explain how the plural was formed.

**Add *s* or *es*?** Give each child two different-colored cards, pink for *s* and white for *es.* Call out the following words one at a time and ask children to hold up the *s* or *es,* depending on which makes the word mean more than one: *hat, dish, bus, glass, cat, mitten, bench, lunch, pencil, girl, boy, lunch, peach, goat, seal, apple.*

**Fix It!** Invite children to correct you with the word's correct inflectional ending as you misread several sentences you make up, such as: *Jane is jump with her rope. (jumping)* or *My dog is biggest than yours. (bigger)*

**Fill-Ins** Write on the board several pairs of sentences like those below. One should have a blank for a present-tense verb; the other should have a blank for a plural noun. Complete the first sentence pair as a model, and then call on volunteers to complete additional pairs of sentences. Examples:
One bird *flies.* Two *birds* fly.
One pony _____. Three _____ trot.
One bush _____. Two _____ grow.

**Make It Right!** Write the following list on the chalkboard and invite children to make each noun plural: *five peach, two dress, nine penny, six pony, two lady, six cat, eight brush, three story, two copy.* Remind children to make any necessary spelling changes before adding the appropriate ending.

**Today or Yesterday?** Say a pair of sentences, such as *Yesterday I worked at school. Today I am _____.* Have children suggest words to fill in the blank, modeling a response if necessary. Engage children in a discussion about past and present. Have them give examples of words that tell about something that is happening now and of words that tell about something that happened in the past.

**Colorful Endings** Write base words like these on the chalkboard: *fly, cry, teach, buzz, skip, work, fish.* Then give children colored chalk and have them give each word an inflectional ending in a different color, making any necessary spelling changes.

**Charades** Use the Picture Cards on page 31 (except those for *tall, taller,* and *tallest*) and have each child choose one without showing it to the class. Then, have children take turns acting out or drawing clues for the picture without naming it.

**Finish the Sentence** Write a set of words like *cold, colder, coldest* on the chalkboard. Have children write or dictate a sentence that includes one of the words, leaving a blank for the word. They can then exchange sentences with a classmate and fill in each other's blanks.

**What's It Like?** Place several objects, such as an apple, a glove, a rock, an orange, and a pencil in a paper bag. Have children reach in and feel each object. Ask them to describe it with a word that ends in *er* or *est.* For example, they could say that the pencil is *shorter than a ruler* or *thinner than a crayon.*

**Can You Hear the Ending?** Read a popular short picture book to children. Then divide the class into four teams, one for each of these inflectional endings: *s, es, ed,* and *ing.* Reread the story and have children stand when they hear a word that ends with their team's ending.

**All Mixed Up!** Write a sentence that includes words with inflectional endings on tagboard, and cut it apart word by word. For example: *I like stories about dancing cats.* (Leave the end punctuation mark with the final word.) Have a volunteer arrange the words to make a sentence and read it aloud. Then have children identify the words that have inflectional endings and say each base word.

# Wordmaker Cards

| | | | |
|---|---|---|---|
| fly | jog | tall | ed |
| rock | try | big | ing |
| fox | rake | windy | es |
| bus | smile | lucky | s |
| puppy | hide | carry | er |
| bunny | fish | wet | est |
| help | stop | hot | i |
| dress | teach | soft | g |
| hop | brush | bike | p |
| wag | bumpy | shop | t |

# Word Bank

Below is a list of words that you may use to illustrate words with inflectional endings. Some of these words are included in the Word/Picture Card set on pages 30–31. Ideas for using these cards and additional cards you may create yourself can be found in "Classroom Fun," pages 23–25.

## Words with Inflectional Endings

**Plurals with s**
apples     girls
books      goats
dogs       mittens

**Plurals with es**
benches    buses
boxes      glasses
brushes    lunches

**Plurals with ies**
*(Change y to i)*
buddies    flies
copies     parties
daisies    stories

**Verbs with ed, ing**
brushed, brushing
fished, fishing
helped, helping
jumped, jumping
looked, looking
parked, parking
walked, walking

**Verbs with ies, ied**
*(Change y to i)*
carries, carried
cries, cried
hurries, hurried
studies, studied
tries, tried
worries, worried

**Verbs with ed, ing**
*(Double Final Consonant)*
grabbed, grabbing
hopped, hopping
hugged, hugging
planned, planning
skipped, skipping
stopped, stopping

**Verbs with ed, ing**
*(Drop Final e)*
danced, dancing
skated, skating
smiled, smiling
sneezed, sneezing

**Verbs with s**
adds       says
eats       tells
hurts      thinks

**Verbs with es**
buzzes     passes
fixes      reaches
misses     wishes

**Words That Compare**
cold, colder, coldest
fast, faster, fastest
kind, kinder, kindest
small, smaller, smallest
soft, softer, softest
tall, taller, tallest

**Words That Compare**
*(Double Final Consonant)*
big, bigger, biggest
fat, fatter, fattest
hot, hotter, hottest
sad, sadder, saddest
thin, thinner, thinnest
wet, wetter, wettest

**Words That Compare**
*(Change y to i)*
bumpy, bumpier, bumpiest
happy, happier, happiest
lucky, luckier, luckiest
sunny, sunnier, sunniest
windy, windier, windiest

## Teacher Notes

**Page 6** See page 4, "Working with the Poem."

**Page 7** *Answers:* dogs, mittens, apples, seals, books, cats, rocks, hats, pencils, girls.

**Page 8** *Answers:* 1. foxes, 2. brushes, 3. buses, 4. dresses, 5. glasses.

**Page 9** *Answers:* 1. puppies 2. pennies 3. bunnies, 4. daisies 5. cherries 6. babies.

**Page 10** *Game Directions:* After children cut out the words, have them arrange the cards face down in neat rows. Have children take turns turning over two cards at a time. If a player turns over a word and its plural, he or she keeps the cards. (For example, baby and babies is a match.) If the two cards are not a match, the player replaces the cards and the other child takes a turn. When all the cards have been collected, the player with more cards wins.

**Page 11** *Answers:* 1. es 2. s 3. s 4. es 5. es 6. es 7. es 8. s.

**Page 12** *Answers:* Across—1. fished 3. jumped 5. planted Down—2. dressed 4. helped.

**Page 13** *Answers:* Children will create *ing* words using robot and word strip. They will write in a word of their choice.

**Page 14** *Answers:* studies, dries, flies, tries, carries.

**Page 15** *Answers:* 2. We planned a picnic. 3. A man was jogging. 4. A boy was swimming. 5. A girl petted a dog. 6. A frog hopped by.

**Page 16** *Answers:* 1. skated 2. raking 3. danced 4. waving 5. riding 6. baking. Children will draw lines to the appropriate pictures.

**Page 17** *Answers:* 1. small: first button; smaller: second button; smallest: third button 2. cold: inside house; colder: fall day; coldest: winter day 3. fast: roller skates; faster: bicycle; fastest: racing car 4. tall: first building; taller: third building; tallest: second building 5. long: ribbon; longer: hot dog; longest: yardstick.

**Page 18** *Answers:* 1. wetter 2. thinnest 3. happier 4. sunniest 5. luckiest 6. windier. What is missing? the sun.

**Page 19** *Answers:* Children will circle the smiling girl, the tallest umbrella, the bigger picnic basket, the smallest ant, the longer leash, and the dog shaking off sand. The beach ball is under the *biggest* hat.

**Page 20** *Answers:* 1. books 2. dishes 3. buses 4. pennies 5. washing 6. baked 7. glass 8. taller 9. fastest 10. bigger.

# Word Cards

| | | | |
|---|---|---|---|
| book | books | boxes | babies |
| paints | fixes | carrying | tall |
| taller | tallest | looking | chasing |
| crying | swimming | dropped | baked |

# Picture Cards

# Observation Checklist

| Name | Writing — Writes words with inflectional endings | Sound to Letter — Can discriminate between comparative adjectives | Can choose words ending with ed, ing in sentences | Recognizes plurals with endings s, es, ies | Auditory Discrimination — Can use words with inflectional endings in context | Recognizes words with inflectional endings |
|------|------|------|------|------|------|------|
|  |  |  |  |  |  |  |
|  |  |  |  |  |  |  |
|  |  |  |  |  |  |  |
|  |  |  |  |  |  |  |
|  |  |  |  |  |  |  |
|  |  |  |  |  |  |  |
|  |  |  |  |  |  |  |
|  |  |  |  |  |  |  |
|  |  |  |  |  |  |  |
|  |  |  |  |  |  |  |
|  |  |  |  |  |  |  |

E=Excellent     G=Good     N=Needs Improvement     R=Reteach